The Poetry & Art of

David Arshawsky

NeoPoiesis Press LLC

NeoPoiesis Press
P.O. Box 38037
Houston, TX 77238-8037

www.neopoiesispress.com

http://www.geocities.com/amuletcypher/arshawsky_index.html

http://turtlemilk.com

David Arshawsky – Amulet Cypher
ISBN10 0-981-99841-0 (paperback : alk. paper)
1. Poetry. I. Arshawsky, David

Printed in the United States of America.

First Edition

I dedicate this book to my family,
and dear friends (who are family to me).

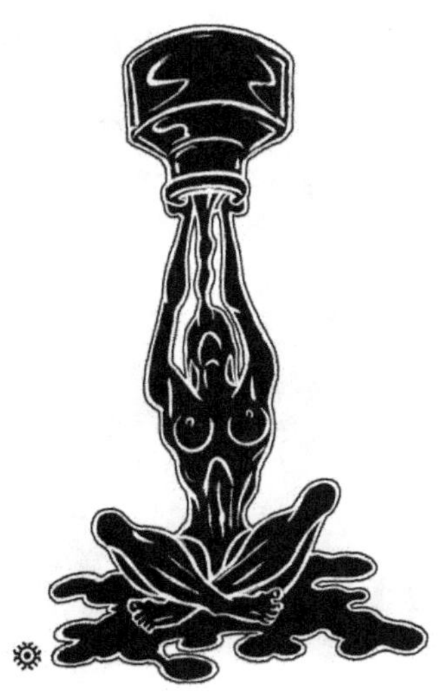

Contents

Foreword

I have been told that before I could talk, I was mapping out unseen worlds with crayon or pencil. Labyrinths, peopled on paper, was how I played. Art has always been the framework for how I experience the mystery, by working in decorating, illustrating and sculpting cakes, as a portrait artist, book illustrator, toy sculptor and designer, and always through writing. Much of my time has been behind the scenes, anonymous, accruing a huge body of work, and stepping out of the shadows now feels right.

The computer has fit right in as a tool in this journey. I remember when I first found the online art groups. There were people from all over the world, posting work and critiquing and commenting. These things we do, we do in the dark and frequently alone. They reflect private, secret worlds and often, will go unseen and unheard. Here bloomed a community, beyond the locality of borders and style, both friendly and contentious, but vibrant and challenging. The artists, poets and writers I have met have changed and stretched my world. It has given me a space to make a ritual of writing and drawing every day.

I am sure that art is a magical pursuit. The time spent experimenting, learning and practicing, at first brings you along incrementally and then suddenly comes the quantum leaps into mysterious yet personal revelations and visions. Doors open and you peer onto the long, strange landscapes of your mind.

David Arshawsky

Transparencies

All these shadows
have soaked into my skin.
Oh, Marta,
you have left me a world
inedible, overdone, smoking.

My feet were blue strangers last night,
my hands couldn't hide the light.
I saw veins and buttergold,
blanket, like gauze to the cold.

I am soon transparent,
unseeable, yet here,
burning things up.
I heard a racket in the walls,
moving, rattling voices.

All who knew my secrets are gone
and I can't speak them anymore,
so they come in dreams,
clearer than my days.

Oh, Marta,
my table is sad.
I saw your beauty till the end.
When you left, I left,
only living in your eyes.

If I can bear to look,
I can see the garden outside.
Nothing made it through
this terrible winter.

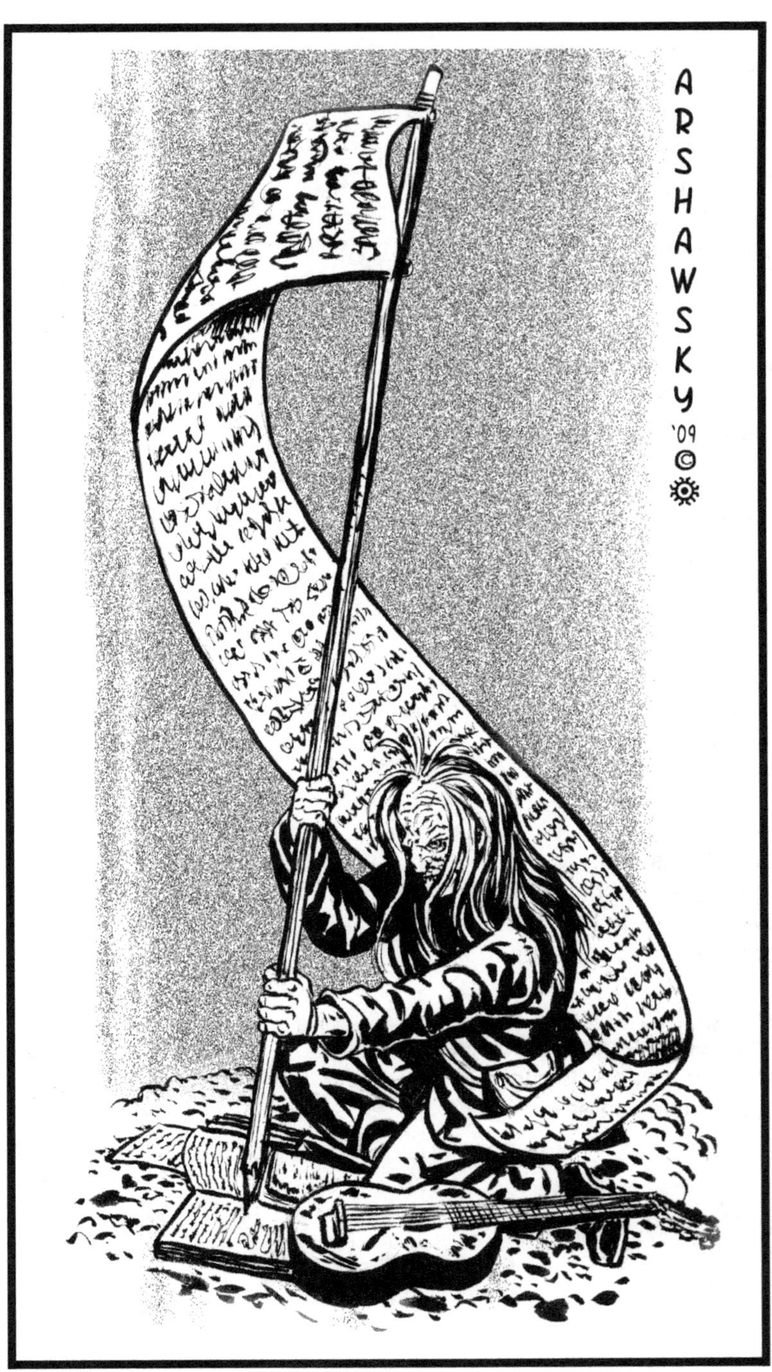
ARSHAWSKY
'09
©

Unaffiliated

This phillum of madness,
our own particular bent
won't assuage neighbors
when the spirits land.

Past the knockdown fence,
all jungle faced
and nightglowing,
when hunters emerge
mirror eyed, stalking.

They look, stare,
- never nodding,
from tidy porches,
in frantic cars, squinting.

In the range of strange
we remain -

Unaffiliated.

Skin

skin, open ended, shines
sunseen, glorious
wrapped like a flag
on a spindly post
hair, tipped electric
skin, like paper written
in ecstatic verse
skin like truth, unadorned
but shining, shining, touched
skin, split down, seamed
banner blooming, bellied out
played like notes on wind
devoid, unarmored, plain
'cept in sun
'cept in sun

Weighted Down

i am in a snow of strings
pointing down

the sway of gravity
i am in a rain of chains

rusty locks
i carry a heaviness of time

tail pinned
tailspinned

too dragged down
to shuffle

now, slowly, comes the sun
a banquet of gods
golden, toss shadows
to the staid and static

butterflies, birds
look like scratches in my eye
mouths move
hands gesture

i am in a storm of dreams
dissipating

the weight of wrongs
i am a fountain of salt

under passing clouds
i hold the heaviness of time

It Comes Like Rain

When the faithful fear,
we will wring our hands
and under tears
Ink will smear.

This night, without candles,
splits the sun's heart.
We will know the dirt.
We will taste the clay.

We will be without the words.
We cannot keep
or force to stay,
the things we lost today.

It comes like rain,
spilling over and away-
The liquor and tears,
the flames of love and youth.

Down, deep beneath,

they seep.

Pilgrim

Standing at the edge of the mawing precipice
wrapped in the crinkle of aluminum foil robes
sucking marrow from holy relics - swinging smoke.

They come, they come, on the tasseled skirts of a red sun.
Forgone heretic scrutinies, the precepts remain unleavened,
a vast thermos brimming, full of black twisted tongued saints
in hawaiian ghost shirts and immaculate adidas, ascend.

Helping the heavy limbed and swollen flock
through the buttered gates of heaven,
buttocks still burning from Satan's rude cavital search.

Here in the swirl, where fingers form of chalk and cinder
and cursed clouds who must remember
dampen the air with sugared spit,
the gelatin globed eyes form, from the silt thick muds.

Bottled lightning breaks in the lapping thick crust.
Heathen hearts compress in the thorny cage of ministried greed.

Coil within cotton, strapped with the weight of blooded letters,
mad incests of a murderous Father,
their prayers, now fossils sunk in stone.

Madrigal

Hands alone, softly set
twine lovely in mine,
breath seen like bellies
shock the morning with heat
acquired a blushing red.

Quietly now, devour the world
in beds of bracken and flame,
eyes a million years bright
ambered honey in tears tangle
some new left love.

Like battle flags up against
such sad decay's bitter divisions
and yet pale hands wander astray
in this early dangerous dark
of breath and softness.

Closely sent whispers
of pliant secrets inhaled,
slowly stirring birds,
the pale light signals
this madrigal's fleeting pause.

Red Tide

They come up
along the jagged coastline,
a winding path
near the end of all hopes.
Look to the west
where looms in the darkness
an abandoned lighthouse,
where wild water breaks
and churns a glowing red.
I saw them leaping
hand in hand over the edge,
down to the phosphorus plankton glow.
I saw lights swoop
from the starry frozen black.
Like dancers they fell
to a shelf of rocks,
hands like children.
Hand in hand
they keep coming
at the end of all hope.
Land's end,
on a shelf of rock.
Red, like petals to the tide.

Creatures

creatures
of skin
of style
to notice

such slow
motion
of grace
and salt

seminal
of scent
fleeting
primordial

languorous long
unnamed
self defined
bursting light

exquisite lines
profound shadows
to drown
or draft

creatures
in eyes
spurred to
reckless notion

abandoned
hollow guise
at barriers
easily crossed

Red Bridge

how i found you
in a spidering oubliette
i didn't read the map
lazily lost
when the hours dropped away
i found
far from everything
the rusty red bridge
spanning the frantic
silent
thick with paint
cooling
under a spider-legged sun
the names unable to hold
on the devil-bright skin
the mayan zigzag
of crooked rooftops
falling away to salt
southward, shimmers
in antiquing kitchens
pale leaves boil
and strange unguents
you barely there
and untouchable
til night

Pockets Full of Leaves

this day burns red
like a tidal swallow, spreads

whiskey winds breathing,
shadows set off running

if i was to touch you,
you would abandon words

and fall
to the liquor of night

in darkness
everything is mine

even now,
your eyes shine wine

red flames
through amber glass

erasing things
like gods and promises

brittle harbors
for creatures of flame

their compact with night
when we fall to tinder

hearts full of fire
pockets full of leaves

Fool's Gold

the sun, then, caught you
shy of water

hissing like a dry worm
kneeling too long

on brittle roots
in squinting sands

moving through minutia
mired in this slag

immense in need
of gilded trains

low slung
with sun cursed ore

when the picture fades
remains the golden frame

and in last breathed joy
you huddled frozen

with something shiny
you feared to question

and hid to hoard

ARSHAWSKY '09 ©

Sweetbread Manna

She was something
kinda rough
and way too young.
She had a solid strum,
purred like a kitten,
came crawling over
when the sun zigzagged home.

Me, too tired for excuses,
swear, it was something I needed.
Locked in my head, lonely,
reasoning that all are mad.

Looking out to disaster
I would walk away,
but not from a couch
and not from that.

I am not a bad man,
but I may qualify.
I never deserved
those hungry, reckless hearts.

All that manna sweetbread
falling on my stupid head,
eating so little.
Some kind of sin to waste
even a mouthful.
How I yearn now
for just another mouthful.

Matchbox

Whisper lightly,
to keep it safe,
keep the light low,
let the shadows hold;
the doors are hot with fire.
Windows will shatter glass,
ghosts walk the hallway
with relentless weight.
There is a secret in this matchbox.
Bones brushed with sulphur
painted yesterday red,
packed too tight.
Too tight to heal,
too hid to steal.
Just to open it up
will set off the spark
that will eat all the darkness
and tear down the walls.
Tonight keeps quiet
to hear the long gone walking.
Secrets spoke lowly
to the ghost of a heart.

Kill the Day

A long road twists out from the abandoning sun,
the land hangs on to the heat, long gone.
The night blooms in a million soft pollen breaths
under the starlight's scattered beauty.

Let's kill the day
and bury it under black water clay
and under shuddering eyelids
churn the day's madness
into a quicksilver elixir.

Sleeping bodies feel the world turning
while dreams dance out like ghosts.
Mad, convulsive, free from reason.
Barefoot, we run through the moonlit phantoms,
the air rich with cooling clay.

The sun's marshal rule
is redeemed only by the soft madness of night
where we touch their faces
with tear wet kisses and longing eyes,
though barely fingertip far.

Words won't explain.
Knowing is enough.

Away

Mouthfuls of light and tint eye wanders
Away

Rain stopped on skin shimmered and toes rippled
Away

My shade, in amber hearted eye, sinks
Away

Child fingers, cold tips, shudder, tighten, turn
Away

Hot heart mists, storm sky passing
Away

My mind reconstructs you, skin and smell as you move
Away

Ask

Won't you?
This will is rusting out bad,
this road is lonely without markers,
this burden has grown so,
just to skirt the devastation of knowing.
Past, with teeth like broken glass,
mutters murders, unending, long.
How heartless to dispatch hope and illusion,
leave them unburied under such a sun.
Just asking, an invitation
to kill what may be the very last.
The very last.
The anger, the hate, the hurt
is what lasts as strength,
as an ant crawling home
under the weight of a hundred murders.

Night Cranes

Silver, in rows of night,
like ghosts to tomorrow,
they notice the disappearing.
The buried land under
the last of the morning mist.
They heard your eyes seeing,
they turned into that silence
as you dragged on by,
clumsy with weight,
unworthy of dirt,
unknown to the sky,
lost in geometries of death.
They are here to say
goodbye to you.

Reaching

I came awake into your eyes
somehow, across this long black forever
out of dreams, awake

See how our fingers pass through
past, yet clear and cool as glass

I reached out to brush
all the fiery dust from your hair
tumbling down, drowned

I saw myself in your eyes, reaching
We of words, shone silence
in this branching, reaching place

Release all forgotten dreams
in radiating ripples, we mixed
like before, like now,
in places we cannot seem to hold

Lashed under this liar's sun
in rushed pages, scripted in fire

I yearn for night's slow forgetting
of all bright lies and awful pains
just may hope to wake to see
myself in your eyes,
Reaching

Under Farewell Suns

Small beauties, in circumspect,
now flood forward in spiced color.
In sun specks, shines this hidden place.
Toes deep, unsandled soles
find this place, unmarked,
unreturnable by will
opens up under farewell suns
of tempered time, twined.
Don't speak of our things, trials and ails,
of tired tales, overtold,
of braveries, either mad or bold.
Shredding banners leave like sunset tatters.
We dance through each other,
drunk and stained in twilight wines,
eating the ancient off childhood's scented hair,
long gone, always there.

Remember Them

All the carnage of time,
and I remember them all.
It's true, it isn't the same
now they are gone.
Whole cities have fallen
away from mind, like dead leaves.
I kept something of them,
little points of style, of options
to living so dry.
They left with their golden luck,
- suddenly gone,
and I won't fret them.
Gorgeous in light,
spun, all changlinged
in cumulous dazzle,
they took nothing earthly,
never believed, never caught with dirt.
The world hunts them dead eyed;
the different, the eccentric.
The others fear what negates them,
what mocks their enduring rot.
Their dead tongue leaflets,
their meat bouquets.
They wear fear like rapture,
annoyed by beauty and excellence,
by the horrible unknowing.
Equating breathtaking to dying,
wordlessness to asphyxiation,
laughter to madness.
Let their fear divert them.
May the mad live on
in the shimmer of truths
in between the lines, the living,
living, dreaming, dreamt.

Now

Now that space has tired,
I stretch out in endlessness
like the rolling shade
that skirts the world.

Now that time has frozen,
in twisted arms locked,
you flicker across my eyes endlessly
and I fill the gaps with cool dark.

Somehow, we passed impossibly near
ripples and math and unfathomed consequence,
now that fire is singular, central,
I see everything in everchange.

Since waterlike, once
warps and envelopes,
like worlds, like visions, like bubbles,
shimmer to the sun.

Unmoving, I am free
from gears and goggles.

Gone

The place where I sat when the house forgot me,
where the sounds of traffic ate my mind,
the coffee table that wants to cripple me,
the walls that didn't care to remember my stupid life's fiascoes.
Like the drip of the faucets,
like the weak flush of the toilet,
I'm gone .. soon!
The window where I noticed the parking ticket
under the note you left,
the dustless spot where my stereo
would be playing pathetic songs, if you didn't take it,
my caved in bed where I won't sleep.
You've finally cleaned, leaving a hollow
like a Tijuana plaster donkey with a broken ear.
I smell the ocean and hear the traffic
and a distant, distant alarm.

ARSHAWSKY '09 ©

The Seven

took the seven down
pico
for a quarter
to the sea
half an hour
to heaven
my brother
and towels
to real waves
endlessly
magically
free
practically
they come in
in threes
starting
when they
curl and foam
and you'd fly
superhero
to shore
all day till
sun's setting
sandy legged
shower pole
shoe shaking
pizza
and watch
the end
beginning
beautiful

The Lost

Missed me,
miss you.
By that map you marked,
dark country abounds.
I walk to get lost.
The world
is still strange,
I am a stranger
still.
Buried foundations,
a hollow hearth.
Drunk from
nature's wild whispers.
When the day finally died,
I was burning.
Thought you might see
me on vague paths,
finding signs,
leaving cairns.
The beauty
unfolding, growing,
in night's clear eyes.
A kingdom to claim,
only for the lost.

Script

in a fever
I saw my hands
in some tossed spot of sun
there, I saw a ripple

the light riding ridges
the light and shadowed lines

I saw something I never noticed
somehow never

what have I been doing
to miss
all this?

like script
of my body
now clear
only readable
perhaps,
in fire

Hotel

I sit in red room,
circled in cigarette snubs
tattered with clippings and bullfight posters,
let the light blink like a mad eye
and the walls thud as someone's head
meets the plaster, in love or hate.
The scratched mirrors,
the cat blood carpets.
Your heels unloaded,
my love disarmed.

Dandelions and Thorn

She remembers
the hard work
all done in smiles,
together.
Comes a sigh.
Yes, there was daily water,
enough for green to open,
the color spilling like children,
laughing,
under shade dancing.
She remembers
me, young years, loving,
patient and careful
on the battlefields of weeds
and thorn.
Seasons came,
full of bright surprise.
The seeds we hid
in mud and sand,
brightly brought color.
Seems I forgot,
forgetting
she remembers everything,
almost always.
Battlegrounds of loss
strewn like wounds.
I have returned
on this late day
to notice
a violet among
the dandelions and thorn.

Norco

Like tires burning and cow drenched mud,
I rolled up coming into Norco
a long tender mile, small flies, I cried awhile.
Just into Norco, I saw the signs turn on in twilight time.
I missed the turn, on fumes I ride,
just passing Norco, the darkness came.
I fear I'm done in the passing lane.
Just out of Norco, you forgot my name,
I disappeared like a small blue flame.

Whispers

cloud's twining strands
script in this new cool

an edge of change
brings color to your cheeks
and heightens eyes
crystal ball blue

crows collect to watch
this parade of dreams

raising higher
on dancer's soles

to read the rose
and spilling purple

stars wriggling
out of the haze

speak for the others
beyond the electric veil
the portends display
in synchronous plottings

here the voices
are all around

whisper and point
the changes come

the blessings and the boon
the things beyond our ken
in changing weather, whispers
unseen, unseen

Sent

These things I throw up,
smoke and spark and roll away,
wobble like a top of a drink.
These things I silent, say,
with my tapping down fingers,
jump up into heads
of, now, somebody else.
What I meant doesn't matter,
as the words born, get fatter,
like water in dry desert
send lichen born flowers,
echo in unmapped grottos
and come back like thunder.
My little, odd whispers,
like a ghostline sketch
on hungry hopes sent out
and back a feast to fetch.

Pray

Hail to the wind,
ice fallen, scatters.
See her blue veined hands
pull a braided rope.
She is curved in burden,
a crucifix knitted on her back,
she pulls a rope tied sack.
Carry the burden
on long nailed bare feet
with the angry sun behind her.
I can't see her eyes!
Hands clasped in prayer,
fear comes like her
on hard dirty feet.
Pray! Pray!
The sky bleeds red.
Red blood seeps
into the newborn day,
the past will not be buried.
See the bloody trail
as the sun burns behind her,
and I can't see her eyes.
Pray ! Pray!

ARSHAWSKY '09 ©

Blink

in that faltered vision
blink in static time
end light, salt water
filial nets in arched delineation

cover in winsome webs
cast straight in willful aim
against the turning winds, falter
plans, man, careening, curved to darkness

to buttress time's scoping blades
with final threads cut, tumble out
past shout or scream
into the blackening ultramarine

only the distant ice stars
quiet our burning cores
and it all grows clear
in unseen colors and distant spores

as all dust conspires to see
and bloom fires

Slits

in absalom
outside of the tea storm
scythe like arms stopped
only the peek
of pulsing light
the violent detail
the rushing of
sun, narrowed

to slits

broken paths silence
turn away clocks
tip down faces flat
the creak of floorboards
on your ghost path
the cavern of bed black
the vial of sleep
life will pile up

under slits

behind interrupted wires
the planet on the ceiling
the spot on the wall
the place in the mirror
the fortress of drawers
a cup of air, closing, circles
waits for water

from slits

Lashes

You, trained in my deceptions,
my arsenal of distraction,
my reckless attentions.

And I, after cursing,
still may adore
what looks like two sunflowers
behind bayonet lashes.

Your beauty overwhelms me,
unaware style, reminds me,
through this odd war.

We bump heads in the hallway,
we still embrace in fond attacks
tied back to back,
we share the same string.

Just fingertips,
bust your glassy surfaces
and ripple back, to something deeper.

I'm on the Sun

I'm dizzy
Can't fall down
I'm on the sun
I'm on the sun
I won't tell you the reason
I can't falter
I'm on the sun
I'm on the sun
Baby, I won't behave well
In flames I resign
I can't fall
I'm on the sun
I'm on the sun
Like cool water dreams
In liquid joy I swim
In a heaven of blue
Their legs kicking
Up to daylight
But the truth burns through
And I can't fall
I'm on the sun
I'm on the sun

Rust

A sad acid
comes in the dark months,
high tension skies
drop in these ragged piles
of orange peel burning.
I have fused where I sat,
I can hear the larvae
pool in my sockets,
the roaches lost in my wires.
I still can hear the servos whir
in diminishing motion,
I can sense the eroding shell
as an acid tear wells
caught falling off stretching flesh
on a mechanical tongue.

Tangled

Mired maps know no home,
entangling our endless conversation.
Now in echoing miles, in expanse and vacuum,
I remember your fingers, the weird ripples in your eyes.
We built in our wildernesses,
megaliths and mazes, paths of math.
Spectacles of heat, how they shimmer and drop
in our cooling twilight, turning
our forever tangle, mapped in symbol signals
still tied to breath, our endless conversation.

This Alone Time

This alone time
in shutdown sunset,
a dark glass checkerboard,
ghosts staggered sidewalks.

This alone time
dies with sunfried, scrambled day,
whispers unforgettably,
turns the littlest lost thing holy.

This alone time
finds death an elegant dancer,
creaks in hallways,
drinks unlit wine.

This alone place
packed with absent ghosts,
fills with black,
disappears under smoky sheets.

This alone time
gasps down streets,
glistens all diamonds
crowded into curbs.

Still alone
finds no place of rest,
no haven or hiding,
no peace from ravenous dreams.

Eric

I told you
my reservations
about the past,
just as you pulled away.
I wanted to grab you that day,
dear friend.

When people go away,
they don't really shrink,
they really aren't smaller,
I have learned this
all too well.

I said
better look at things anew,
tomorrows bring surprise,
but you left
sending dust devils swirling.

The gun
never looked right in your hands.
I'm sure it was easier
to look into that dark space
than to hurt another.

Your heart never stopped,
I feel, in that place.
We came too late,
as you leapt into the past.
I pull you into every new day,

though lightly,
like a faraway spider web kite.
When people go away
they don't really shrink.
This I have learned.
This I have learned.

Three Bad Prayers

Three bad prayers
steepled under rain,
bent to the wind,
bitter in defeat.

The silent bell sways
as dust fills
long gone footsteps,
the keyless lock.

The eyes of peeling saints,
cold cracked pools of wax,
the hollow shed spider skins
left sagging on dusty webs.

Three bad prayers
unheard from bitter bit lips
under dark rafter rivulets, fall
like a broken black rosary's beads.

The taste of one's own tears,
the hording of pain,
eyes shut yet restless
in dungeoned dreams.

Unheard.

Oblivious You

dogs hear me
when I call your name
cats open one eye -

in your weird solitary world
barely anything can penetrate
through the fog and static

and me, in madness, moan
scribble stark sigils
move my fingers
classic symptoms
for sugar pills and shocks

clad in cotton balls
you are shielded
from my arcana

spirits sympathize, eulogize,
catalog my sighs
send you to fill my eyes

just a preferred madness
to take up the time
to replace the space

to burn away
the things I need to do

- and you, oblivious you

White Petals

I will see your skin
like a white petal
held before the sun's bright light
and crush the tender lines
in fragrant demise
against the rough contour of my face
and breathe a full field
of wind shimmering flowers;
miles and miles,
in sunbright breath.

Dancing

No one believes I am a dancer,
yet I whisper round the dark,
step between sunspots,
mimic branches and bracken,
cup a sullen sun,
zigzag the rain,
shadow the stamping shoe,
pulling the shadows into day,
twirling rainbows from stone,
doing the ruin,
kicking out barking dogs,
dipping out of disaster,
I have been dancing for years.
- The music in my head,
I have been dancing for you,
though you say ducking.
My hands - my hands
being things,
singing words and lines
best not spoken,
though, through body,
articulate enough,
holding, hiding my own secret beat,
I have been dancing for years.

Changed

It's transforming time

And now I see
I am something new

I'm old

Something fresh,
In pieces

A remnant of yesterday,
Yet more

Look at my sparkles,
Only in the dark, show

And sublime
In that bitter defeat,

I find the key
Like ship nearing the sun

I glow etheric,
Bright

Trailing wisps
Of youth and madnesses

Gravity gone
Elsewhere
For heavier souls

I step off
Onto playful winds

We Are Allowed

we are allowed;
see the bare beauty in it.
these reckless hands may breach
to a sleepy song of apparent lies,
notes to the near nuzzle a tilting ear.
the transparency of clothes,
the sly inhale of line and implication.
we are allowed the brazen kiss,
lingers lazy to shock subdued,
gifting this marvelous mistake.
let the analysts argue it's priss portends
a dance unlocked in midspin
dizzying out to another,
amidst low laughs and blush.
these redlined chapters torn
never tumble, never reach regret.
the plans outlined assured our demise,
yet those salty lips found our all
and left us, blessed us gone.

Breathe

Breathe
and see
like sleeper's trembling eyes,
visions thrown into the sun,
the wakeful walk inside their heads.
Breathe some air that flows
apart from your little nightmares,
from off of snowy heights
on the tail of a Thunderhead,
the razor sharp sun,
the purple veil of space.
Breathe the fire of the world,
step away from your weighted shadow.
Breathe the beginnings,
breathe,
release your reasoned shade.

Silence

Here at the tips, at the buds,
let the blue pinwheels spin backwards
into the soft graded silence.
Tempered color cooled in fire's absence,
the day's words like colored sticks,
like festive kindling.
Brush away the caul and submerge,
like clattering bubbles spent,
sent to the arid day,
down below, here below,
sitting with silence.

Daydreams

Here in the drag of the long day,
against the slavery of the clock
chopping up the day's moments,
while the world's in its tick tock lockstep,

I'm sinking into amber in a wild backstroke,
and through the rippling smoky depths
I might hold a moment so rare
that its minutes set the world in dog years.

The sheerness of your blouse, my hand,
the miraculous soft bloom of your bones
and your hair, the smell of You
leaves the world procrastinating its dumb end.

I recline and summer clarities mosaic
blooms medallions of light
whose radiating sunlit barbs
turn the trudge away.

Sight

Pried from sap or sediment
or tears and sentiment,
my vision blurs to the light,
bends crystals like amulet cyphers.
And I thought you stood over my bed
in yesterday's shadows
and scent deserted flowers.
I squint to see you in shards of light,
pray for day to leave
the dark to sheathe
my sun blind world.
Pass away to see
you here next to me.

Clowns in the Night

Clowns in the night, lose noses in shot glasses,
forget to remove their big shoes,
smile in horror, can't remember jokes.
Clowns in the night, sit in front nude women
who are worried about animals,
have small cars that don't work,
have restraining orders against them.
Clowns in the night, dream of busting up heaven,
cannon shot, with tiny, tiny wings.

Witness Protection

He was hung on heaven,
tossed the book of numbers,
tucked into the bindings
he borrowed from his aunt.

Count the burning pages,
like tears they bloomed in heaven.
Count the empty spaces
in the parking lot of bliss.

Stripped of evil leisures,
the check will clear tomorrow.
Qued in dour parade,
trying not to touch the ground.

Cherubs made of saccharine
clatter down like hellfire hailstones
on cookie cutter tombstones
all staggered in the mud.

Pillbug

I can make my fingers move like worms,
my dirtknobs hang low on my dirt map head.
I huddle against the curved greasy light.
Your plastic sack hints of smoked meat or rolls of lint,
hubris buntings draped in sleeping snakes,
head scabbing under the low asphalt sky.
Little pillbug, plow the crust in coiling depths,
in displeasures, nodding to navel,
another sleeping world.

Drapes

The street lolled like a grey tongue,
nothing left to say that wasn't taken away
and the black boned trees, bereft and crooked,
wait to take her gnarled hand in the bitter winter light.
The children sound like rusted wheels on a coach delayed.
Waiting, waiting, she puts up drapes and warms the kettle.

Drink and Go

My suit wants to stretch out to the sky,
Bijou, my long lost love -
my tears break the sun.

Your skin, from the earth
rich and rolling, like the gentle hills.

My liquor, I spill recklessly.
Drink, my friends,
deeply drink, in the earth.

Keep me up a little longer,
I have nothing more to lose
so I am off to find you

now, as the mud warms
and buds turn pale to colors

as hopes warm the icy waters,
as sun caps the salty waters.

My tears, I spill recklessly.
Drink, my friends,
no stronger brew can I lend.

Send up flowers bright,
to see me go.

Sun

Here in the sun,
all butter melted yellow
and swirl frothed clouds,
our wigs bust out
and swallow the sky.
In swimming pool blue
and rippling sunlight,
spring's tender breath
fills our sails
as we glide
in this sunlit reverie.
All dreams
are remembered and shine.
Sun stand still
and stay, linger,
in our bright warm day.

Wire

We are connected by wires
All the dust and distance

We are connected by wires
We are constructed of memory

We change every day
Variants in every blink

As particles pull apart
We are connected by wires

Sleeping in white noise whispers
Diverted by pause and diversion

I remember the contrast of our skin
Remember the unsaid

I feel the tides of aura
Leap towards you pulling

Everything unlikely in this distance
Falters hesitating, this pause

Yet signals radiate
This truth indicts

We are connected by wires

My Place

such tender hopes
unfamiliar to me

in lost angles of light
i keep looking to see

undefended hearts
unnerves me

that you leaned
toward me

and saw something
i have never guessed

done without
for so very long

i have made my place
in solitude

and you

Metal Butterflies

When the aluminum spring has unwound,
and the summer's heavy rust climbs the sunhot copper stalks,
the burnished petals bend open wide
with antennae stamens, protract, perceive,
a starward static they receive,
and from colored zircon coils you soon can pry
the precious metal butterflies.

Hands of My Father

I pull aside my fear, heavy like a rough hewn stone mask,
and look down at the silent shudder of screaming life
that ripples under muting skin, legs kick for a hold,
the mind fights to enter the diminished flesh.
I, holding the strongest hands, God's hands,
kiss the veins and try with whispered promises
to turn his head as the sunlight
grows in heat on his beautiful shoulders,
like crowding love's sweet soothing hands.

Matchsticks

I saw the socks they couldn't hold,
the lacy, frilly kind.
Your calves were lean and held to bone
in tan skin's moistened shine.
Behind your knees, dissed my ease,
and upwards the thighs did flow.
Under windswept dress I did my squinting best,
only a sliver of light did show.
Those matchstick legs did strike a flame
in this crude heart's desire,
and looking at your sunlit gap,
I found myself on fire.

Falter

Another letter to you
And I falter

The sounds withhold
All this distance

With thoughts
Smoking, pluming

Masking
Those few true things

Devicing
Odd intentions

Not of speaking
But quiet near

And the unclear horns of voice
Those flags of word

Those paper thorns
It hides my needs

Of silence
Of bumping foreheads together

And faltering
In silence

Together

Old Friends

I won't ask you where you've been,
or speak to hear sounds
or fly or fry at silent spaces.
Roam free in the bounty of friendship.
I don't check your pockets,
or remind you of time,
oblivious of sins and sums.
A smile ...
we just continue
where we left off,
though years and years ago.

They Keep Coming Up

They keep coming up
skinny and delicate,
awkward and shy,
and then, shimmering in beauty
with some ancient grace,
shining ankle and sloping neck,
blossoming in curve and swerve.
I am lost in young women,
like a sailess raft
on a swelling tide.
They lift me up
and gently pull me down.

Model Prisoner

My idea was, perhaps lost
when the paint was dry
or when I hid that hand print on your sweater.

I never understood why you tried
to hide your nipples.
I showed you mine
and they were fine.

It's strange the way beauty cannot see itself.
I would have brought candlelight

had I known
how mean the fluorescent tubes would lie.
I kept a discerning face,
like a man deliberating

when all I wanted to do
was press my face
onto your lean belly
and breathe you in.

I would have destroyed that mirror
where vanity's madness abolishes
the unaware grace of beauty.

And you were half out the door
already sliding on the sweater,
unaware of my ever guilty hand print

waving good-bye.

ARSHAWSKY
'09 ©

Workhorse

In this terrible, terrible cold,
my grandma is my scarf,
my dad, gloves,
my grandfather, boots.
So much is must,
so little rest, so I move
with workhorse ethics.
There will be no memory,
no forgiveness, no quarter in defeat.
My hand must be steady
to take the task.
This winter world
in death dreams, cold.
I take on their madness,
hoping it won't stick.
When I catch my sleep,
somewhere, somehow,
I will forget their paper faces
and return to the warmth.
A loving armor that endures,
protects me. I will find a place
outside wind and woe
and smile, somehow,
then laugh, perhaps,
forgetting the reason
and the reason not to.
They surround me, light,
respite from tomorrows'
fights and trials.
Bundled up in love
the strength will hold.
I will face the wind
like they did,
- Walking

First Cry

i suppose i was heard
but unfound.
strange,
i was hoping
to find someone, waiting.
listening in the dark,
the sound was gone,
just my own,
alone.
attended to
by efficient hands,
i was still waiting
when the lights went out.
i was still hungry
after the bottle emptied.
i felt that ache,
felt the room empty.
waiting,
long after the light went off.
listening for that sound
long after it stopped
looking for me.

This Town

This town is full of crosses.
Where can a little bird find a bloodless branch?
Come sundown, I find no walkers, no loud talkers,
no night dancers, no tears, no bitter love.
My arms unlinked, my song seems my own.
I would take the ashes from the east,
set a table for shadows
and spill some schnapps for a stranger.
My door always ajar, my table with extra chairs,
I would bargain with the wind
and sell shadows wholesale.
I hear a world, just behind a sundown shade.
Dead tongues live and make jokes for crying eyes.

Monastery Mists

Sisterly, no, fingers touching.
I want these words to hide, unseen.
Black benign, cooling miles
dipping time, reflection sky, wavers.
Cooled sunset, reddens down.
Abandoned stones, release
lapis lazuli lizards,
taste the night coming.
Ice edged rivulets
tap chill tip roots.
Once a monastery, now wild,
the mists are pure desire.
Unchained spirits passing
into a forever, beyond before.
I want this whisper to be wind,
evermore so, flying across the
living, votive night.

Hurtful House

Father Hatchet rests his blade
in the shadow of Sister Shy and Brother Hate,
while Mother Blind scrubs stains in Cutlery Kitchen,
while you peel the paper in the Hallway of Echo.
Here the door is always locked,
the heart beats as loud as the footsteps
and the fears hold their breath, once again.
Children, hide from the shadows
long as the lies, in this Hurtful House.

Teeth of Love

A rose in bloom, will swell the senses,
shock the memory's arcane bouquets,
pull you close, and close your eyes.
This is why to heed my advice...
First the color, then the scent,
then stumble, know thorn's grief.
Like passion, after the tongue
comes the sharpened teeth.

The Swirling Dust

Look over the green
And pretend to see

You
and
Me

Today can't imagine
Resting here together

In pathless pastures
Now under new roads

We are in the clay of yesterday
Knowing the difference

The tidal change
A moment staying, swaying

Beneath the muddy rain
And tomorrow's yesterday

The final dance plays out

Victim
and
Victor

Will be indistinguishable
all
In the swirling dust

The Moon

It's always been the moon and me
throwing shadows in my path,
stark, her awful aura, bereft of bird.
Brooding judgments adorn the lower world,
her hands wring over black waters.
My regrets haunt me
in this shatter light vacuum.
She shames me with a name
and I can't run fast enough
to catch the trailing sun.

Violence

The echo of meat fills the gap,
like red feathers, wet with salt.
Who controls?
Like a pierced beetle spinning on two legs,
maniacal clockwork, crippled,
fed a fist, blindly thrown,
praying for meat, for the holy sound of glass
or the damage of a crippling wall.
The unhealing gut wound
spasms outwardly in bone orbits,
while all masked in mirror
soon shatter into unfamiliar cries.

Mirror

As if my skin alone could hide me,
I envy the mirror, hard and smooth,
invisible and contrary,
I look into my eyes
and find darkness and faces I dread,
my choking bloodline,
my mother's fear.
Here in the dark,
my skin won't protect me,
as all eyes are that mirror to me.

The Rub

Snail trails scooting
In hightailed hungers

The blood ripened root
Bent in a dull dry plead

He rides the tailwinds
Of a narrow escape

A wrong that closed your wet eyes
When tears were unexplainable

And to short eyes the limp
Betrays your rhythm

Closing curtains in the dark

ARSHAWSKY '09 ©

Darkness Seeds

That is why there is darkness,
so not to know,
so not to end.
These names we learn,
these cages we grow into,
this monster we ride
is the great tide of us.
As we turn in the light,
we are moving off away
obscured in night.
Something found in the breaking,
something glimpsed
in the swirling dark,
said in mute hand,
sung in body mystic,
clearly in the abstract,
horns and haloes blurring.
In the falling, rises
a guidance star
in the center of our imprisonment,
like a beacon sun.
Do we despair
to capture endlessness
awakened in child night, gasping?
The end of ends,
the gravity of loss,
the journey away,
pulled in magnetic array
into unknown familiar,
into truest aspect,
awakens the seed.

Muscidifurax Raptorellus

Just a fly for swatting,
in quick prayer hands, closing,
sends a tiny angel twitching -
then another maggot to the meat.
How lightly it touched your eyes,
its filth and tiny rainbows lit.
Always aloof, circling askance
and rubbing hands of prayer.
The pleasure of pestilence,
The theft of temporal sleep.
When the dreams come no longer,
baby gets a bed and breakfast.
Start and end the short desperate day,
hands rubbing out another carnal prayer.

Rain Seeds

let it go in winter mode
this child will see more summers
it is the fresh rain, accepted
that will replenish, that will seed
it is in death's arms that we will dance best
dip and swirling spin
wreath flowers, fallen, are best to kick
kissed toes will lose the cold
let love under the blankets
let it be traced by nose and tongue
to the flower of your core
the welcome of your comfort
will find new fires
eyes alive to this new day
songs back from the silence

Sun and Wind

i still hear the whisper
a day away,
forced into waiting,
i noticed

i no longer fought the sun
or sought the shade,
no longer counted strides
or set my mind afar

then came the wind
softly down from high
with kindness, cool

people passed
unabstract, real,
eyes alive

this is the world
to walking real,
the smallest courtesies
keeping the world whole

what pushes us along
so fast to crash
into darkness
alone?

in our self sealed heads -
outside, the clouds
are on the move, always,
slowly

too skewed to symbols
to see
the holiness
of small things, passing

the discomfort
of elements
out of our control,
dies

and lets us touch
sun and wind,
receives us

into the element

still feeling whispers
a long day away,
waiting, noticing

roofless,
under moving skies,
reconciled to the sun

Unchainable

take him from the mesh
cull him from the stitch
we all know where the book bent
that love could usurp kingdoms
that would vanquish all this hoarded fear
was hardly heard under cannons crash
what silken cloth stretches
separating us from truth
look at them cluster
gobleting blood and tears
hoping for malfeasance
praying for blood to spill
into the letters, into the lines
cans and bullets, bunkered and buried
what we kept was the cross
and left love unchainable

Blue Bottle Buried

Bitter water will keep us alive.
Glass black rocks serrate the land from sky.
Gone the roads, signs shot hollow.
The Lord has peeled off the rocks, wholly so.
The shovel and pick, rusting rot, lain and lost.
Snakes settled in their ghost gone holes.
Down, the rattle of rollercoaster winds,
savage and iconoclast, mustang wild.
Cumulous gods collide in vast array,
sun vain, assiduous in battles, above.
There is a blue bottle buried far below,
a gift, a glint, from sun to scaling sands.
A red fire, darkened down, done with desire,
close to raw rough gold, forever hid.
Body gone ,the breath ever goes on,
under every sparking star, alive, aware,
and beyond dark borders, under smoke and glow,
they bloom yet, wrapped in scenting skin,
drunk with blood, stuck to shadows, stand.
Lips of liquor, taste, and fear
to squint and see, the long off black of lost.

Wired That Way

I am a serious man,
finding meaning
outside of beauty
withstand the quiet
pour myself
into hours alone

Still ~

The depth of color
flashing in your eyes,
breathe and hold
to catch your scent,
the delicacy of your fingers
pushing back your hair

Dismiss ~

A sober stasis remains
from madness, dragged to daylight,
a strength from going alone,
no debt or hated favors.
The simple things of men,
reclaimed freedom, undiscounted

Forgotten ~

To the line of neck and shoulder,
the shock of ankle and heel,
curling toes in open shoes,
the soft hair kissing your ears,
the back of your knees,
winds and dresses

Gone ~

With logic and proverb
it comes in close,
remanding you
to the kindness of death,
the liquor of youth
drunk from young lips

Away ~

Wired that way.

Acknowledgements

I would like to thank Dale Winslow for being such an excellent and discerning editor. I want to relay my deep appreciation to Amanda Pierce and Erin Badough for their careful and excellent work on the layout and look of the book. I am grateful to Mark Weiss for his elegant graphics and design work and his friendship. I want to thank as well, the online poets, for sharing their work and thoughts and providing an atmosphere that is challenging and inspiring.

NeoPoiesis
a new way of making

in ancient Greece, poiesis referred to the process of making
creation – production – organization – formation – causation
a process that can be physical and spiritual
biological and intellectual
artistic and technological
material and teleological
efficient and formal
a means of modifying the environment
and a method of organizing the self
the making of art and music and poetry
the fashioning of memory and history and philosophy
the construction of perception and expression and reality

NeoPoiesis Press
reflecting the creative drive and spirit
of the new electronic media environment

www.ingramcontent.com/pod-product-compliance
Lightning Source LLC
LaVergne TN
LVHW020648100826
845148LV00012B/2384

* 9 7 8 0 9 8 1 9 9 8 4 1 1 *